# DOKTOR BEY'S SUICIDE GUIDEBOOK

# DOKTOR BEY'S

# SUICIDE GUIDEBOOK

INTRODUCTION AND COLLAGES
BY DEREK PELL

DODD, MEAD & COMPANY · NEW YORK

1 2 3 4 5 6 7 8 9 10

ISBN: 0-396-07439-1

Library of Congress Catalog Card Number: 77-80597

Printed in the United States of America

DEDICATED TO MY WIFE YARRA,
THE SUICIDE MUSE.

# CONTENTS

# INTRODUCTION

IT WAS in 1948, during a sojourn in Egypt, that I came across this strange, neglected masterpiece. Sitting in a crowded cafe in Cairo one evening, I observed an unruly cluster of intellectuals engaged in heated debate. At first, I attributed their exuberance to the powers of *m'hashish,* but soon learned they were under the spell of something far more potent: a handwritten manuscript on self-destruction! As the tattered pages passed from table to table, the patrons' reactions ranged from amusement to outrage. When, at last, I was given a section, I read it eagerly–experiencing both delight and astonishment. *What incredible mind could have conceived this work?* People throughout the world were seeking a way out, and here was a volume filled with answers! No shabby moralizing–just sound advice and encouragement. In all my travels, I had never come across anything similar. I was instantly determined to meet its creator.

The following morning, I set out by camel in search of Doktor Bey, the enigmatic author. He was rumored to be a deranged obstetrician, a pornographer, a deformed pharaoh. But when, a week later, I finally located him living reclusively in a tiny shack beside the Nile, he appeared most ordinary. He was, quite understandably, reluctant to discuss his book with a foreigner, and threatened me with a scythe. However, when at length I succeeded in persuading him that I was not a government agent in disguise but an admirer, he invited me into his study for a talk.

He explained that the *Suicide Guidebook* was but one of a series of texts on a wide range of controversial topics. "I've written a handbook on abnormal sexual habits," Bey announced, with a wink. But he had long since abandoned the idea of publication after a hostile reaction in Cairo. A conspiracy, he implied, was out to destroy him, to keep his works from reaching the world. I quickly offered to take them to a publisher in my country, and the Doktor agreed, remarking: "The people need this book–not another *guru!*" I nodded. Misery was widespread, an epidemic threatened . . . here was a solution for the masses.

He opened an old trunk and removed a pile of musty manuscripts, thrust them into my arms, wished me luck, and shoved me out the door. "Remarkable man," I mused.

Back home, the reception of the publisher was disturbing, causing me to realize that my role as agent for Doktor Bey could be dangerous to my well-being. Perhaps the world was not ready for such sagacity.

Now, twenty-eight years later, his work is being recognized in America. Unfortunately, the author is too old to travel to the United States and too bitter to accept the inevitable forthcoming awards. But the path of genius is seldom smooth. I only pray that readers will appreciate the information contained herein, and take the Doktor's words to heart.

Derek Pell

# PROLOGUE

EVERY man, woman, and child has suicidal tendencies. A shocking declaration? Perhaps. But nonetheless, a plain and simple truth.

The latent urge to take one's own life manifests itself in many forms—a faraway look in the eyes, a constant frown, a peculiar smile, a penchant for late-night strolls—as well as in such common expressions as "I can't go on like this," "I wish I were dead!" and "I could just shoot myself!" Behind the faces and words lies a dark reality.

We are, each and every one of us, susceptible to the idea of *getting away from it all.* The modern age has left us feeling insecure and obsolete.

The reasons for suicide are countless: unpaid bills, in-laws, politics, war, lima beans, bad wine. These are only a few of the causes. Yet it would be foolish to suggest that one must be deeply depressed in order to contemplate the deed. Nothing could be further from the facts. While it is true that many a morbid soul is prone to participate in self-kill, others slay themselves for the sheer art of it—noble motives, sport, or even a stylish climax to a life of adventure!

In spring, when a young man's thoughts turn to self-destruction, he is immediately confronted with an awesome dilemma: *How should I do it?* "With an axe?" he asks himself. "A rapier? A ghoorka sword?"

The young man is consumed by confusion and, judging from the statistics, will choose the wrong method. In short, he will fail.

This guidebook was written for both the chronic and potential suicide. If read and studied carefully, it will make the job easier as well as more rewarding.

Remember, it's *your* funeral.

D.B.

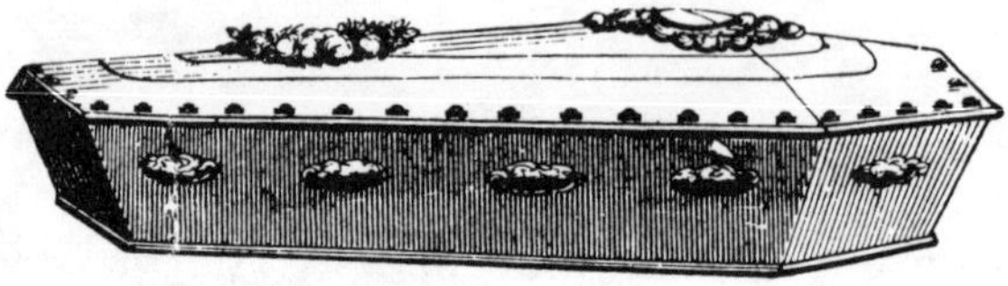

# THE POTENTIAL SUICIDE

Here are a series of individuals prone to self-murder. Study the faces. Try imitating their expressions in the mirror.

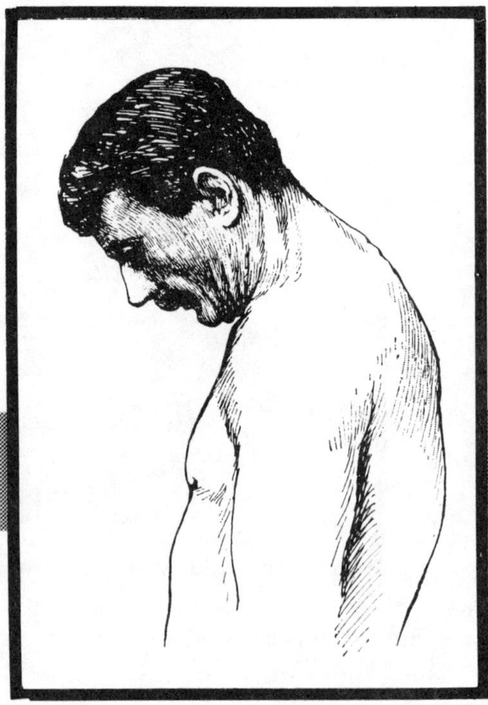

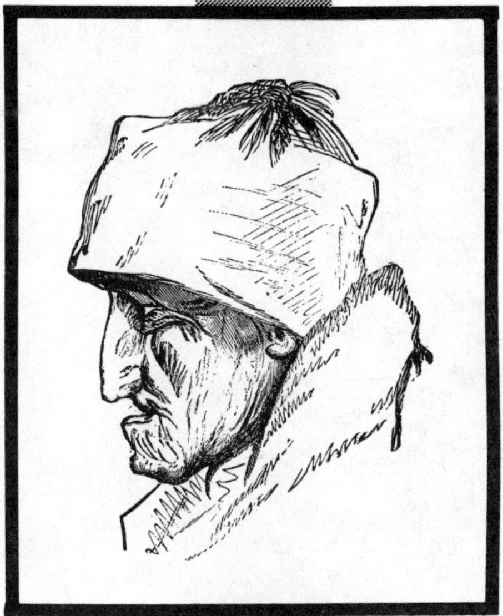

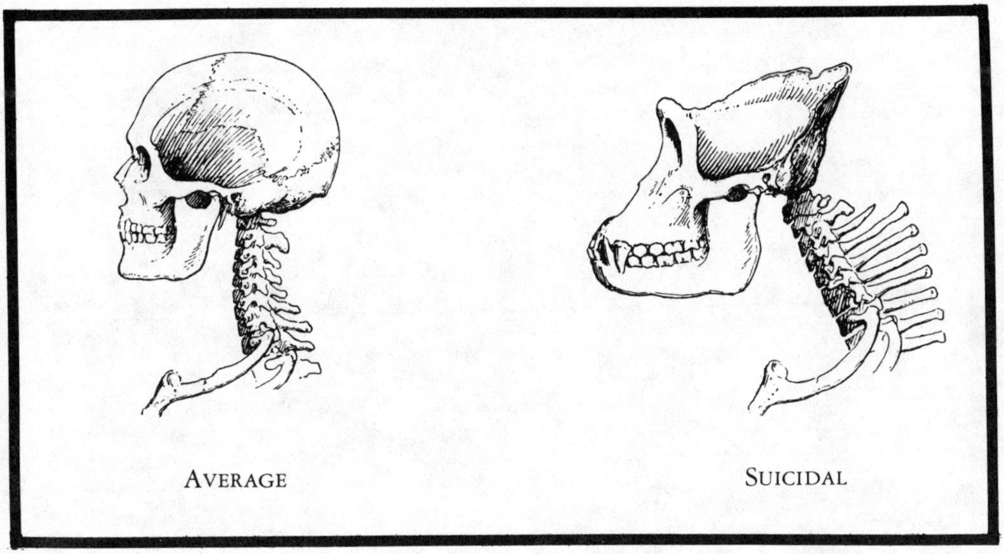


"Am I a potential suicide?"

One who asks this question is usually not. Nevertheless, a foolproof method of identification is the bone structure.

QUIZ: FIND THE POTENTIAL SUICIDE

Only *one* of the six figures in the above illustration is a potential suicide. See if you can select the correct one.

# THE POSE

The contemplation of suicide is an art in itself, and should be treated as such. Take time to discover the pose that best suits your personality. If possible, do your brooding in public for maximum effect.

# COMMON CAUSES

FAILURE ON WALL STREET

Especially popular in America in 1929.
And sometimes even a group activity.

A POOR PERFORMANCE

Onstage or off, this may simply be the result of miscasting. Still, the result is the same.

## MATRIMONY

Marriage can often lead to suicide for at least one of the participants. Frequently, however, it is a terribly slow process. Not recommended.

TRIBULATIONS IN COURT

Such outbursts as that pictured above may lead to confinement and, at length, to a search for the ultimate escape.

## POLITICAL HARDSHIP

Advocating a return to slave labor or an excessive tax will lead to instant loss of office. But avoid rural areas where mob torture is prevalent.

UNPOPULAR

To be shunned by one's companions at sea has led some unfriendly souls to their rope's end.

# THE FAILURE

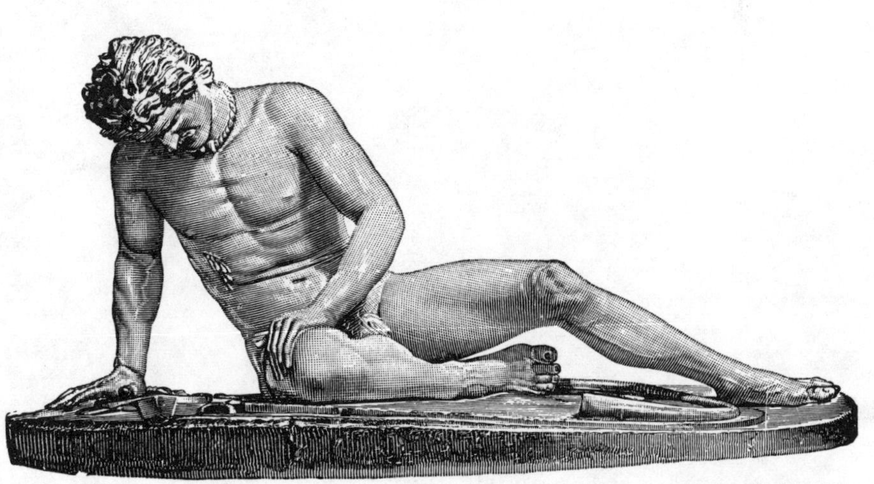

The suicide failure is destined to exist with the knowledge of his ineptitude, unable to communicate the depth of his dolor to his loved ones. Inevitably, he lives a long and wretched life.

## GRANDSTANDING

Low jumps usually result only in slight fractures or sprains.

## HEELS OVER HEAD

A notoriously poor method because someone inevitably interrupts the performance to make the rescue.

In a fit of melancholia, the man above made the mistake of instructing his servant to douse him with liquid hemlock. He lived to be ninety-three.

THE JOAN OF ARC SYNDROME

Because this woman placed her fagots improperly, she did not prove as combustible as she had hoped.

At the suggestion of his mistress, this man jumped into a vat of boiling goat's milk. The resulting third-degree burns so repelled the mistress that she departed, leaving no one to assist him to his end.

HANGING IN THERE

Bedsheets or other lifelines should be avoided at all costs, as there is often a tendency to hold on until help arrives.

The most common cause of failure: panic.

One should, if possible, be photographed prior to the last act, thus preserving one's final pose for posterity.

# THE ART OF SELF-DESTRUCTION

## *THE CLASSIC LEAP*

Since the beginning of time, millions of men and women have jumped to their deaths from mountains and monuments, off bridges, statues, and trains. They have also tumbled into volcanoes, oceans, and ravines. Indeed, the fatal leap has proved to be the purest form of self-destruction, unequaled in simplicity and style. What mortal has observed the plunging of a bird toward earth and not felt a rare sense of exhilaration?

Though a few misguided philosophers have confused man's urge to self-destruct with a desire to sprout wings and fly, nothing could be quite so naive or preposterous! The earliest experiments with flight were little more than thinly-veiled vehicles for doom—the quest for a graceful escape from an inhospitable planet with all its attendant responsibilities and horrors.

It is not uncommon nowadays for youth to reject the experience and advice of their elders. Yet it would be foolish for anyone seriously concerned with a means to end it all to dismiss the classic leap as an archaic compromise, rather than to see it for what it is: an artful and time-tested solution to one's woes.

## THE LOVER'S LEAP

Since the invention of the automobile, more couples are driving to their doom rather than holding hands and jumping. The latter method often ended in last-minute separation. The auto enables lovers to cuddle in comfort, while ensuring a "till death do us part" goodbye. Recommended for romantics.

"JUMP! JUMP!"

Crowd support can be a welcome addition to the experience, spreading gaiety and a sense of adventure.

One of the pitfalls of leaping is the Good Samaritan. Always check the area to make sure there is no one to catch you.

## LEAP YEAR

This historical anomaly occurred in England (once the world's capital of suicide) in 1802, when an estimated ten thousand persons plunged from a certain cliff in Brighton. The English last celebrated this phenomenon with an orchestrated economic disaster, although their position as the leading suicidal nation has since been relinquished.

## POISON

Perhaps the most dignified of all methods, this can be enjoyed with a last-minute supper.

THE PISTOL

Quick and effective.

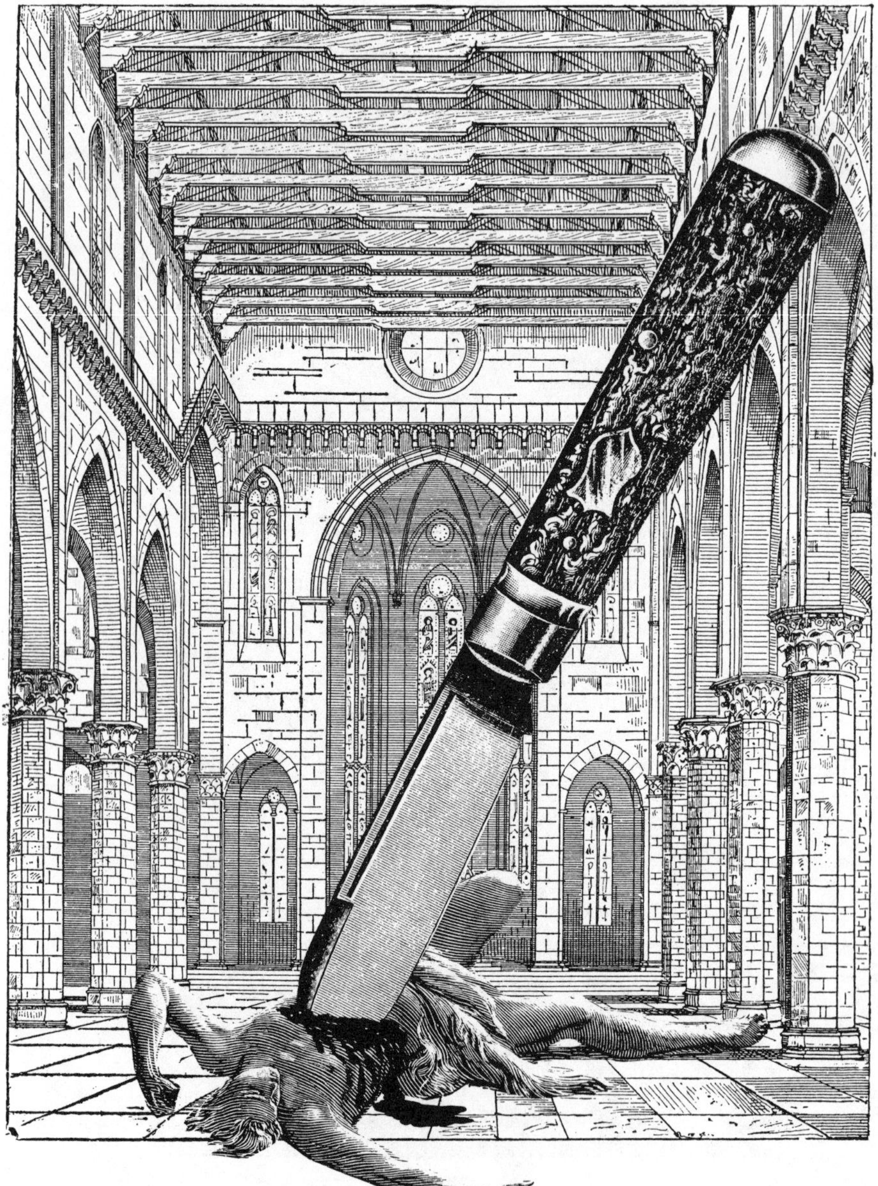

THE KNIFE

Effective and quick.

If you wish to hurl yourself from a moving carrier, be sure the vehicle has attained a sufficient velocity to make the dive fatal.

## LAST STOP

Dashing in front of a moving train is not a bad ploy, particularly if it is recognized to be a protest against poor service and eventually benefits those left behind.

## THE OVERDOSE

Narcotics are a favorite among young people. A wide variety of drugs is available and, unlike poisons, are said to produce pleasurable side effects, commonly referred to as "the last picture show."

## RECKLESS DRIVING

A perfect mode for the moody. Especially popular on the Continent.

## DROWNING

Perhaps the most traditional method, one which offers a wide variety of settings as well as an almost infinite range of opportunity.

. . . such as being hauled at the end of a rope. This usually requires having accomplices on shipboard, however, or must be carried out late at night.

DRIFTING OUT TO SEA

One should not begin too far inland, as this poor lady did, for fear of rescue. Instead, pick a swiftly flowing tributary or stream with direct access to the ocean.

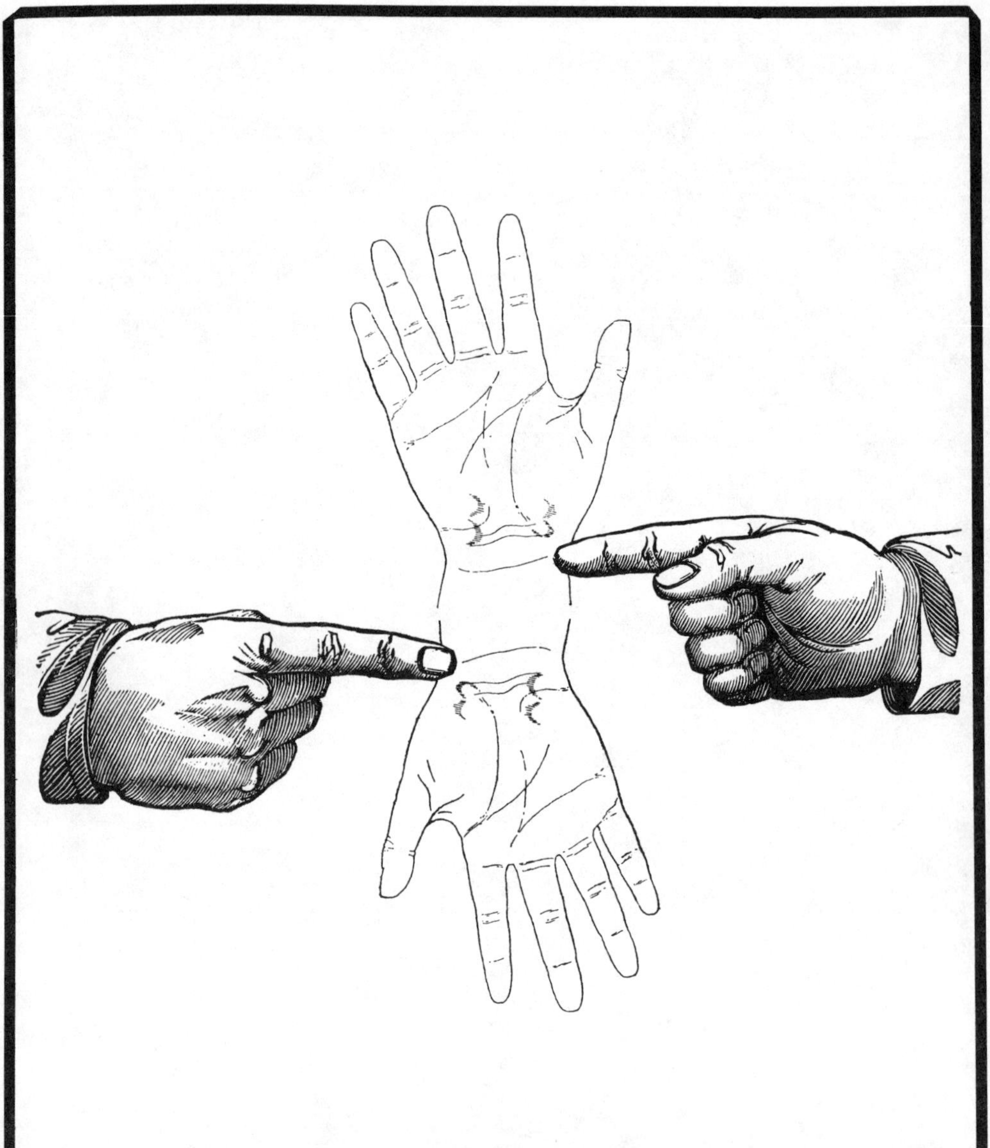

## SLITTING THE WRISTS

More often than not, this common procedure results in failure, leaving the self-murderer limp-wristed and, worse still, *alive.* Since the scars are slow to heal, the unfortunate bungler is obliged to wear gloves, indoors and out, or suffer the scorn of his community and be branded a hopeless dilettante.

For a safe, effective suicide by this method, just follow the simple rules listed on the following page.

## HOW TO

1. Use a freshly sharpened butcher knife or small axe, though when employing the latter, be careful to stroke *lightly.*

2. Draw a line on the wrist(s) just below the cuff-wrinkle (see diagram on preceding page).

3. Hold your implement in whichever hand is most comfortable (if you cannot decide, use the eenie-meenie-minie-moe selection process), and position the sharp edge of the blade four inches above the line you have drawn.

4. Take a deep breath.

5. Now, as gracefully as possible, slice with the blade across the line, penetrating the flesh by at least one quarter of an inch. The stroke should be even. *Do not use a sawing or hacking motion.*

6. Bleed.

## LIVE WIRE SUICIDE

Also known as "The Fourth of July," this technique is popular among exhibitionists.

## THE CATAPULT

Exhilarating, but requires several helpers.

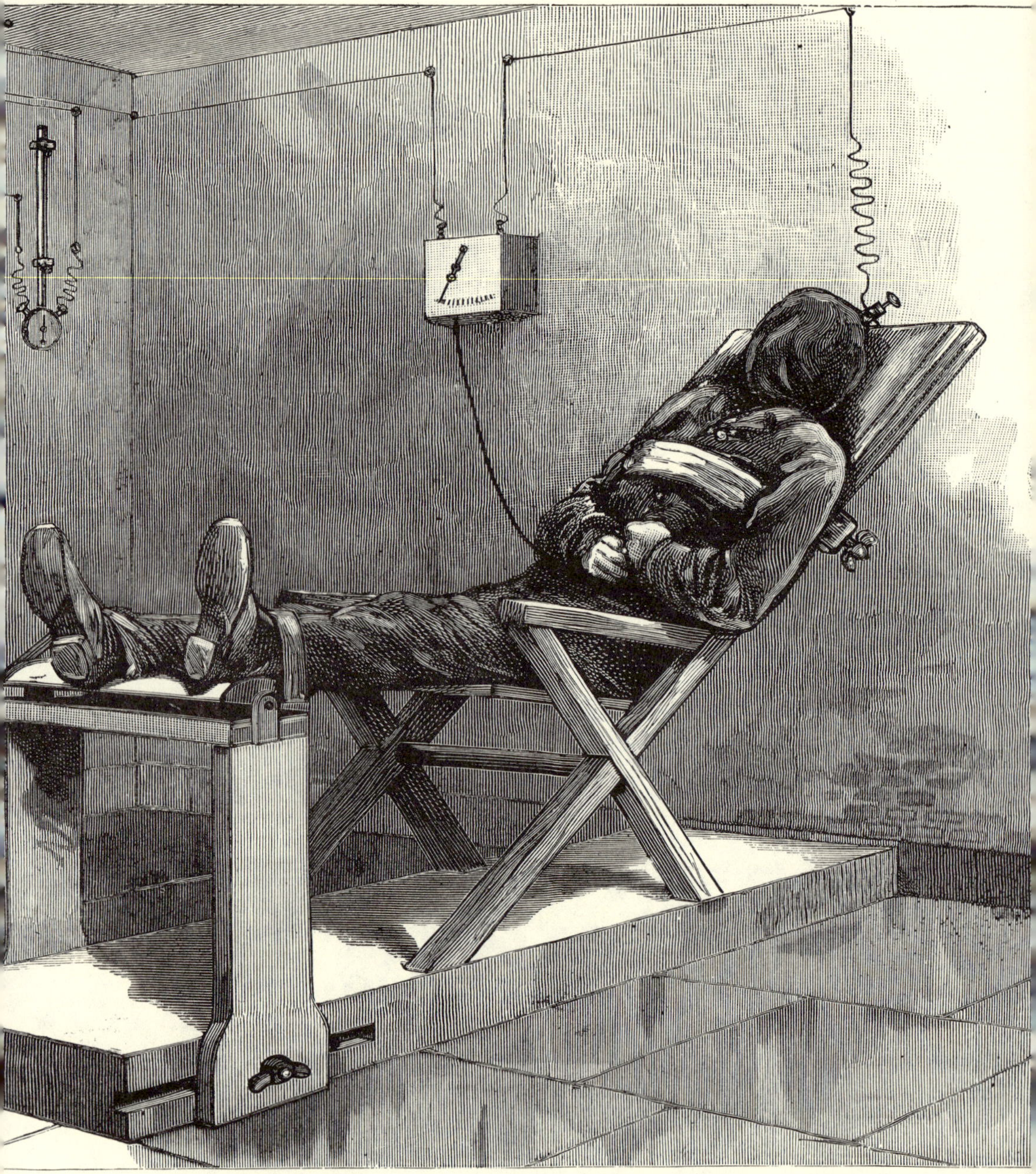

## SELF-ELECTROCUTION

This somewhat complicated arrangement was devised to avoid the uncouth "fan-in-the-bathtub" method. Certainly a stylish and rewarding exit for the mechanically-minded gentleman.

## SINKING

This requires the cooperation of a hostile navy and may prove tedious if their marksmanship is poor. Not recommended.

## GROUP SUICIDE

Although killing oneself is generally regarded as a solitary act, group suicide has been steadily gaining popularity throughout the world. However, it is frequently destructive of property and requires an even number of participants.

## BALLOON

Unpredictable wind currents and dangling ropes often intervene, causing the plunge to appear awkward if not fully planned.

## QUICKSAND

A slow but nonetheless effective method. Should be avoided by individuals prone to indecision.

SUICIDE BY HIGH EXPLOSIVES

For thoroughness, this method is difficult to duplicate, but one must beware of innocent bystanders.

# ACCESSORIES

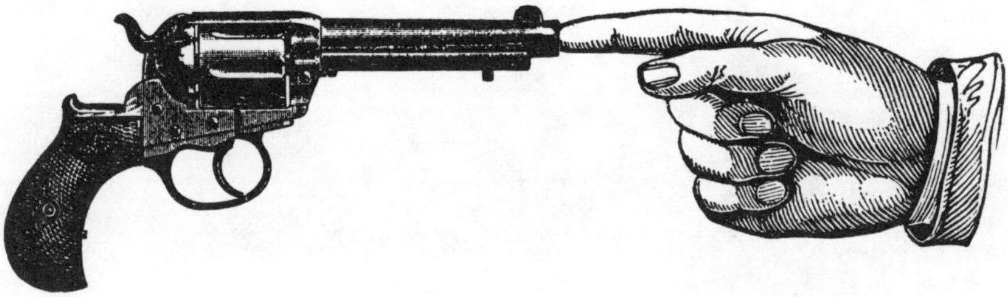

SELF-SCREWER

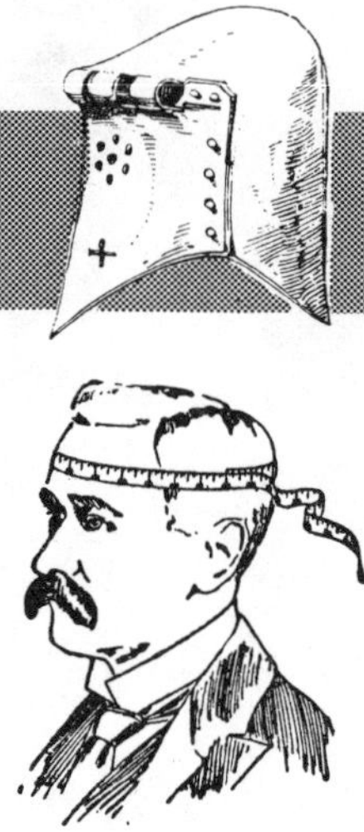

AIRTIGHT ARMOR

HEMLOCK HUMIDIFIER
(with mouthpiece)

THE SNUFF BOX

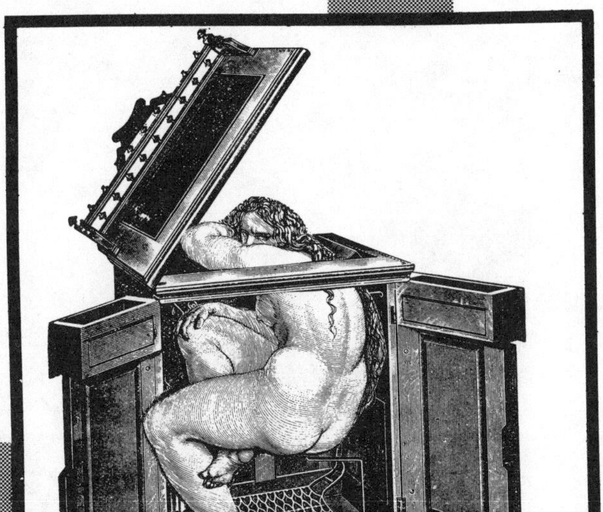

TYPEWRITER

SMOTHER CUP

WORM CAKES

ALACK-RACK

SUICIDE SHOES

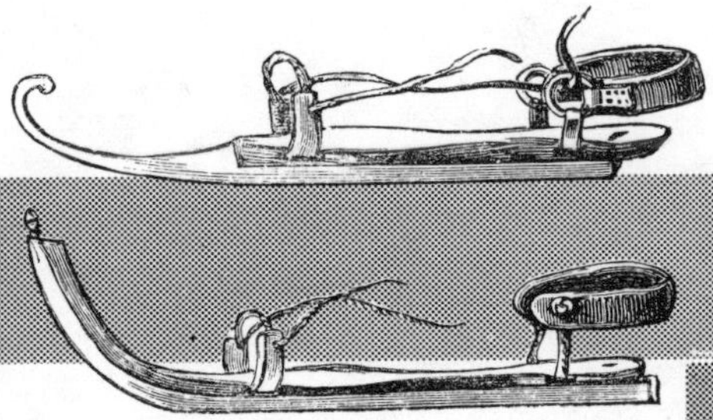

DR. LYON'S DIE-WITH-A-SMILE
TOOTH PASTE

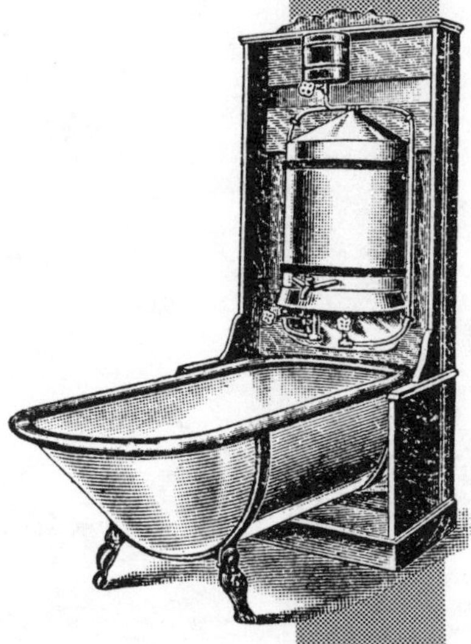

ACID BATH

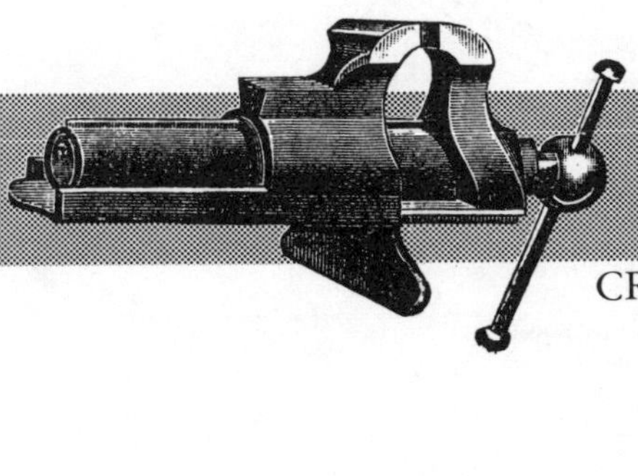

CRANIAL CRUSHER

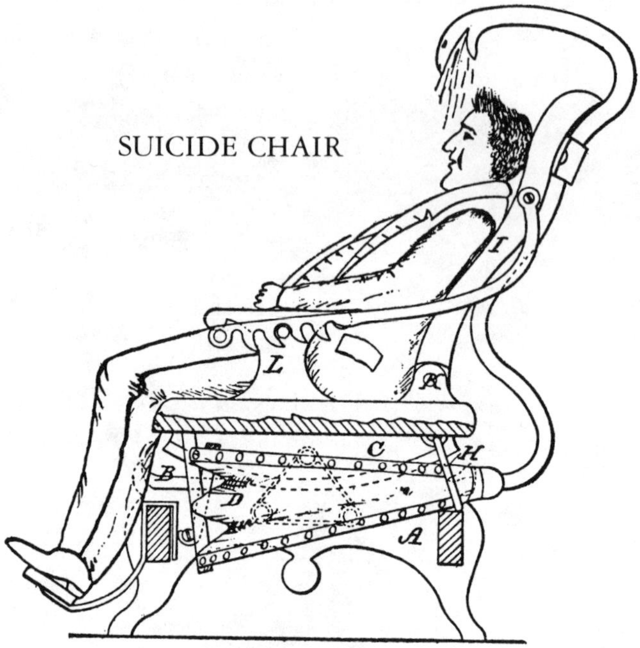

SUICIDE CHAIR

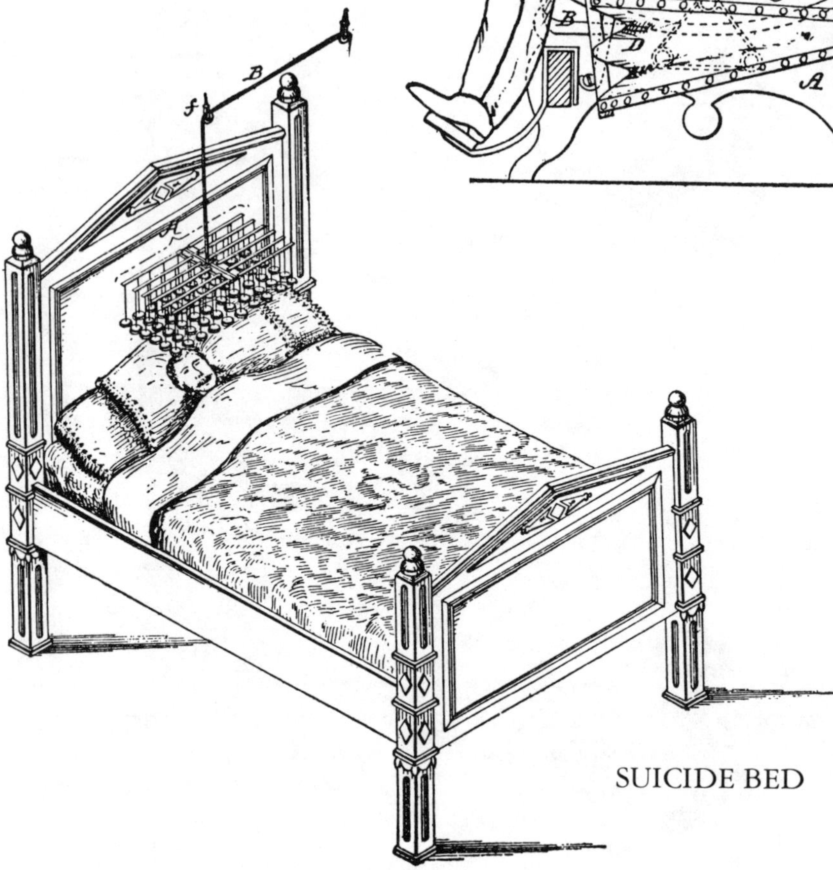

SUICIDE BED

SUICIDE DOLL

Can be purchased in any large city store or country mall. Most useful as a study for developing and perfecting techniques.

MEMORIAL

# THE SUICIDE NOTE

Here are ten tips to aid you in writing your suicide note, a particular often overlooked.

1. Use of the first person is generally preferred.
2. For maximum impact and credibility, always write in the past tense. (*Example:* I *was* a failure in business.)
3. If you are without family, friends, or even enemies, address the note "To Whom It May Concern."
4. When possible, use a typewriter. Far too many notes are indecipherable.
5. Keep a carbon copy in your pocket, in case the original is misplaced.
6. Do not concern yourself with the "beginning-middle-end" rule. Just concentrate on the *end.*
7. Keep in mind that these are your *last words.* They should be commensurate with your social position. They should reverberate in the reader's mind! Avoid such cliches as "Goodbye cruel world" and "To be or not to be . . . " Strive for the poetic.
8. Self-pity, slang, and obscenity are acceptable.
9. If artistically inclined, attach a self-portrait.
10. Be brief. Nothing is more boring than a long goodbye.

# THE HALL OF FAME

SENATOR TELESPHORE CLEMENT (R)

Elected to the Suicide Hall of Fame in 1867 for taking his life with a flagstaff on the floor of the United States Senate during a filibuster.

HANS VON SNAREPOPPIN

Elected to the S.H.F. in 1850 when, after being found impersonating a nun, he strapped himself to the clapper of a large Lutheran church bell.

## SIR ALFRED P. SPRATT

Elected to the S.H.F. in 1903 when, as a judge, he pleaded guilty to the charge of bribery and sentenced himself to death by El Miste, a volcano in Peru.

# MAYOR OAKEY HALL
# &
# THE CITY ADMINISTRATION OF
# ROTON, NEBRASKA

In 1898, at the height of a grain-feed scandal in the little town of Roton, Nebraska, Mayor Oakey Hall and his entire administration committed group suicide by smothering themselves at the bottom of a grain silo. A unique contribution to the annals of suicidology.

ALBERT AND EVELYN LaRUE

The youngest members of the S.H.F. and the only siblings in the group, they earned their place when, recognizing with horror their lustful and unnatural passion for each other, they committed suicide by attempting to walk from San Francisco to Sri Lanka (formerly Ceylon).

Dolor animi gravior est quam corporis.*

*Pain of the mind is worse than pain of the body.